# NO ROOM FOR DOUBT

## SELECTIVE ESSAYS FOR YOUTH

# NO ROOM FOR DOUBT

## SELECTIVE ESSAYS FOR YOUTH

Safvet Senih

Translated from Turkish by Omer A. Ergi

TUGHRA
BOOKS

New Jersey

Published by Tughra Books
345 Clifton Ave., Clifton,
NJ, 07011, USA

www.tughrabooks.com

Library of Congress Cataloging-in-Publication Data

ISBN: 978-1-59784-248-8

*Printed by*
Çağlayan A.Ş., Izmir - Turkey

# CONTENTS

# FOREWORD

Doubt and suspicion have existed all along and they will continue to exist. But these days, generating doubts and suspicions about faith is like a contagious disease, and right and wrong seem to have swapped roles. Unfortunately, materialist arguments against faith are presented under the name of science and knowledge. Debating issues that have not been proven is considered normal; however, continuously producing doubts on established truths is a contradiction of rationalism.

Other nations of the world that took the West as a role-model in science and technology have also begun to emulate its non-religious stance. Doubts, suspicion, and destructive criticism are produced everywhere. Questions and arguments such as, "Who created God? Should a person who had not seen the Prophet be held accountable for his/her rebellion? Is punishment by eternal hellfire justifiable when the human lifespan is so short? Does God need our prayers? Why did God create Satan?" now inhabit the homes and lives of all believers. "Approaching everything with suspicion" was a natural reaction against the scholasticism of the past. However, such a method of thinking does not work for Islam, which embraces human nature with all its faculties.

The author of this book, Abdullah Aymaz has been tutoring and guiding hundreds of students for many years. In this work, he tries to address the intellect, the heart, and the soul of his readers in order to alleviate modern doubts and suspicions.

We hope the precious services provided by Abdullah Aymaz will be appreciated and praised by the future generations. We pray for the aid of the Almighty for the continuation of such helpful works.

M. F. Gülen

Art points to an artist, embroidery points to an embroiderer, and the universe points to God. He has created everything; then who created him? If He is the cause of existence, then what caused His existence?

a. Logic states that it is impossible to embrace an unbounded chain reaction in regards to cause and effect. There has to be a point of beginning. For example, the last car on a train is pulled by the one in front and that particular one is pulled by the one in front it and so on... However, the locomotive pulls all of the cars. It is self-powered and the logic of pulling stops at the locomotive.

b. A created entity cannot be a creator. How could an entity that has come into existence through creation, possess the power to create the existence?

c. Self-existent power cannot be compared to obtained power. For example, human beings possess a relative self-existent power compared to a pen. A person can move a pen from one location to another. However, when a person moves from one location to another, we cannot say, "it is impossible for you to come here, so, who brought you here?" Another example of this line of questioning is: if we ask someone the following question, "what carries your head." He may reply by saying, "my body." If we then ask what carries his body, he will reply, "my feet." Once again, if we ask what carries his feet, he will probably say that the earth carries his feet. At this point, it would be illogical to ask what carries the earth.

Just as the example, God is self-existent, therefore, one cannot ask a question like, who created God?

d. It is irrational to ask a Muslim this question. Muslims believe that God is eternal and everlasting; He does not beget, nor was He begotten; He is a Supreme Being who possesses the qualities of Unity, Oneness, Sublimity, Incomparability, and Ascendancy. Perhaps, such a question could be asked to an idol worshipper. However, asking a believer a question like the one above would be the same as asking a human anatomist "where are the wings on the human body?" Therefore, placing God in the same category as His creation would be quite incongruous.

The Almighty explains His oneness in many parts of the Qur'an. For example, it is stated in the Surah (chapter) Al-Imran (3:18) that God (Himself) testifies that there is no deity but He. God forbid, if there were others, could He have denied their existence?

a. The question above also indicates one of the miracles of Prophet Muhammad. According to one Prophetic tradition, he stated that such a question would be asked in the future.

b. The person who asks such a question initially accepts that God is the creator of the universe and then questions the cause of His existence. This means that the person is referring to God as a creator and a creature within the same sentence. This is a contradiction within itself.

Another illogical aspect of this question is that it suggests that God submits to the laws He has created Himself. All creation is bound by the physical law of cause and effect. The reason for this is we are limited by space-time. God, on the other hand, is the creator of space-time and matter. Therefore, His existence does not depend on these properties. How could the creator and implementer of such physical laws as cause and effect submit to His own laws?

---

What will be the condition of those who have not heard the Islamic call to faith? Are they responsible for the religious obligations prescribed by the Qur'an?

God does not deprive anyone of His revelations, verses, divine messages or mercy. This is quite evident in the following verses:

> *...there never were there has never been a community but a warner lived among them.* (Fatir 35:24)

and,

> *By God, We certainly sent Messengers to the communities before you* (Nahl 16:63).

The Holy Qur'an has not explained the stories of all the Prophets that were sent: *Indeed, We sent Messengers before you; among them are those (the exemplary accounts of) whom We have already related to you, and among them are those (the exemplary histories of) whom We have not related to you* (Mumin 40:78).

God sends revelations and inspiration to every living being:

> *And your Lord inspired the (female) bee: "Take for yourself dwelling-place in the mountains, and in the trees, and in what they (human beings) may build and weave* (Nahl 16:68).

Sometimes, revelations can be a book brought by the angel Gabriel; sometimes, they may be a light that God shines in His servant's heart. At times, they could appear as a sense of tranquility or serenity in the chest. Divine revelations can also reflect in the hearts of human beings as wisdom, truth, understanding, peace, fear of God, and righteousness.

Anyone who has opened his/her heart to the divine truth must have received some form of warning or a blessing from God.

Even the gaze of a Bedouin at the heavens in awe of the Divine has great value in the sight of God. Monotheistic elements found in different communities suggest the fact that God's Messengers once taught them about truths. For example, the Maw-Maw tribe of Africa believes in a creator that possesses the following attributes: He is one; He does not beget nor was He begotten; there is none like unto Him. They call this creator, "Mujdee". According to Maw-Maw people, this creator cannot be seen but he manifests himself through his actions. He hears all prayers and provides sustenance. Lightning is his sword and thunder is his walk.

The interesting thing about these descriptions is that they remind you of the Surah Ikhlas. Where could they have obtained such knowledge unless there was a Prophet in their history?

On the other hand, it is a fact that none of the earlier teachings have retained its purity.

*God burdens no soul except within its capacity* (Baqara 2:286). God makes this clear in the Surah Isra when He informs us that He will not hold accountable those who have not received Prophets' teachings in their purity. This means that there is a great difference between a community that has not received the divine messages and us, who were blessed with the Holy Qur'an.

---

You say that the Qur'an and the Prophet are blessings sent upon humanity. You also say that they will testify against us if we do not live according to their teachings. This means that if divine books and Prophets were not sent, human beings would not be punished in hell. Then, how can they be a source of blessing?

God has planted many capabilities and talents into the hearts of human beings. These are seeds that exist in our very nature. Holy books and prophets have brought divine truths that will help us cultivate and nurture these positive capabilities that help human beings to surpass the angels. If prophets and divine books were not sent, these unique human qualities would remain as seeds and never flourish. For example, even if we have one hundred date-tree seeds in our possession, they will remain as seeds unless we plant them into the soil. However, when we do plant the seeds, perhaps eighty seeds may decay and perish, but if twenty seeds flourish to give us twenty date-trees, we will not be in deficit. On the contrary, we will be making a great profit because twenty trees will produce thousands of fruits and seeds. Moreover, it is the quality that counts not the quantity. According to this logic, a tree is more precious than one thousand seeds.

Using this analogy, we can conclude that one Companion of the Prophet or a scholar of the Qur'an is far more valuable than thousands of people like Nimrod, Abu Jahl, and the pharaoh. The reason for this is that the Companions have exceeded the angels and became the brilliant stars of humanity.

---

### What wisdom is there in the creation of Satan?

The rank and spiritual level of human beings increase through a struggle with Satan. Human beings improve themselves by resisting the temptations offered by Satan. Furthermore, worthless and abased souls can also be identified through the temptations of Satan. This world is a realm of assessment. Just as intense heat separates gold from other elements, the whispers of Satan help to separate and distinguish diamond-like souls from the coal-like ones.

---◦∞◦---

**If Satan is a means for human beings to make progress, then why will he be cast into hellfire? Should he not be rewarded for his services?**

Deeds are judged according to intentions. Satan's intention is not to help human beings excel but to deceive them and to guide them into hell. In the process many human abilities and qualities improve and develop. We have to remember that by attacking certain bird species, hawks help them to develop their flying abilities and maneuvering skills. We do not reward the hawk for the services it provides…

---◦∞◦---

**Religious decrees state that it is forbidden for siblings to marry each other, yet we know that Adam's children married each other.**

a. God creates many things from a sole entity. It was God who created all human beings from Adam. Moreover, Eve was also created from the same clay.

b. Beauty and ugliness or right and wrong are defined according to God's decree. From a physical point of view, there is no difference between a man's being intimate with his legal spouse or his committing adultery. However from a religious perspective, the latter is a sin and it necessitates punishment both on earth and in the afterlife.

Since God is the owner of divine wisdom, everything He does has a purpose. What He commands becomes a thing of beauty, and what He forbids becomes evil. Time, space, and everything in them, together with the physical laws they depend on, are in the hand of God Almighty, who does everything with perfect wisdom and knows His creatures best. Thus, he knows the best concerning the interaction between the limited number of the first human beings, as well as the principles befitting the psycho-social case of those who increased in number and faced new conditions.

We must also remember that all new establishments have certain temporary principles in their constitutions. These principles usually become amended in time and some of them are abrogated. Perhaps, we should approach the issue of early human society from this perspective. The six essentials religion can never be altered; however, details of some practices may vary depending on the time of arrival of the faith and the medium. Practices can only be changed through divine wisdom. As the human population increases and societies differ, some practices will also be modified.

c. Prophet Adam's twin children were cross married with children born after them. According to sayings of the Prophet, a divine decrement was implemented right from the beginning, and this was a ruling forbidding twins from marrying each other.

d. Distant marriages help a more balanced distribution of wealth. If this was not the case, people would have wed their children so that the wealth remained within the same family.

e. Another important moral and ethical issue is the fact that the children of Adam did not know they were supposed to marry each other until the divine ruling came down. If the religions did not forbid this type of marriage, there would be many indecent interactions between the young siblings of today. Therefore, these days no one bears salacious thoughts regarding this matter simply because religions have set their boundaries through strict principles, rulings, and traditions.

---

History suggests that America was discovered by Christopher Columbus. If all human beings are the children of Adam, then what is the origin of Native Americans?

a. It is a geological fact that at some point back in history, the continents split like a jigsaw puzzle. This is an indication that human tribes may have separated through this particular phenomenon.

b. Another geological fact is the freezing of the Bering Strait. Certain tribes could have easily crossed over from Asia to North America.

c. Historical evidence also suggests that Norwegians, Vandals, and Muslims had traveled to America prior to Christopher Columbus.

---

**What would you say to those who claim that they should not be held responsible of religious obligations because they had no say in their creation?**

a. This claim is quite illogical because human beings did not exist prior to their creation. They were not forcibly taken away from another realm and were brought here. God has created them from nonexistence and blessed them with amazing biological and metaphysical equipment. The properties of ego and self awareness were granted by God. Even in this modern era, human beings do not have full control of their own being. How much control do we have over our emotions and reflexes? The existence of a constant divine knowledge and power over our own bodies cannot be questioned. Otherwise, we cannot explain the phenomenon of our heart beats and the maintenance of the trillions of living cells in our bodies. This means the true owner has total control over His possessions. What is a human being and on what grounds does he/she have the right to complain about self-existence? The true owner of all matter is testing us within the boundaries of existence which He has created and rightfully expects nothing but total obedience and submission.

b. Existence is a blessing in its purest form. On the other hand, the fundamental nature of nonexistence is evil. The evidence is that all beauty depends on existence. How could there be beauty in the absence of existence? On the contrary, all evil and wickedness originate from nonexistence. Whenever we come across an evil act or some form of wickedness, we realize that there is something missing or absent from it. For example, appearance of a tumor or a goiter on the human face may seem as materialization, in reality it abolishes the perfect symmetry that is evident on the human face; therefore, order and beauty becomes nonexistent. Similarly, darkness, which represents evil, occurs only in the absence of light. Light represents good, and its existence could be considered as beauty that prevails over darkness. All forms of evil originate from nonexistence. This means a person, who claims that he/she did not wish to come to existence and therefore I should not be held responsible, does not have any idea about the beauty of existence.

c. Imagination is the obedient servant of the mind and intellect. If a question like, "Would you prefer a life of royalty for a million years, and be perished for eternity at the end of the term or would you prefer to have a troublesome life but live eternally" was put forward to our imagination, without doubt it would choose eternal life over eternal punishment.

d. We are quite aware of the desperate efforts of the people who are given the death penalty to have their sentences converted to life in prison.

e. All indications suggest that human beings want immortality. Moreover, eternal existence is an obsession. If human beings had the power, they would kill death itself, terminate nonexistence, and close the doors of the grave forever. Questions such as this one usually come from those who wish to free themselves from responsibility; they are nothing but excuses.

---

**The Holy Qur'an mentions the name of Abu Lahab. Is it suitable for the Qur'an to talk about such insignificant individuals?**

a. Small incidents mentioned in the Qur'an may sometimes seem insignificant, but they are examples of significant general rulings and decrees. Without question, the fate of all those who oppose the truth and rebel against God has been and will be like that of Abu Lahab. This is a reality that has repeated itself throughout history. The Abu Lahab incident is a small sample presented to us; however, it symbolizes the nerve-end of a general rule.

b. A powerful king will be concerned with the actions of all those in his kingdom, even if they are peasants. For this reason, the Qur'an gives examples even about bees, spiders, and ants. This means that divine revelations will have stories about all of God's creatures and servants. As it mentions Prophet Moses, it will also talk about the pharaoh and, of course, Abu Lahab.

c. Another important lesson to be derived from the story of Abu Lahab is that he was the Prophet's uncle who renounced God. The incident is a significant example, teaching us that all those who stand against the truth will suffer a horrible fate even if they are the relatives of the Prophet.

d. There is also a miraculous divination given by the Qur'an here. Although there were significant foes such as Abu Sufyan and Khalid ibn Walid, the Qur'an did not mention their names, but talked about Abu Lahab, who ended up dying as an idol worshipper and an enemy of God. The others eventually embraced Islam.

### Why does the Qur'an talk about a spider's nest?

The forty-first verse of the Surah Ankabut has many important truths:

> *The parable of those who take to them other than God for guardians (to entrust their affairs to) is like a spider: it has made for itself a house, and surely the frailest of houses is the spider's house. If only they knew this!* (Ankabut 29:41).

a. First of all, it is a beautiful analogy that explains the fate of those who befriend other than God. A spider's nest is the most unsecure place of refuge. In fact, it is a trap for those innocent visitors who wander into it. It is a deathtrap even for its own kind. Some female spiders will eat the male following the ritual of mating. As its young ones grow to a certain size, the mother will eat some of them, and some of the young will be eaten by the others. The position of those who turn away from God is exemplified in an amazing manner in the verse above.

b. Another marvelous sign provided here is the fact that the Qur'an mentions the flimsiness of the spider's nest but does not mention the web. Today, we know that its web is four times stronger than any other string that has the same thickness. Therefore, it is the nest that is weak and not the web.

c. The phrase at the end of the verse, "if they but knew" suggests this was a scientific knowledge that would be discovered in time. Without doubt, these biological mysteries are continuously being solved by the scientists of today.

d. Since the verse was revealed in Mecca, it also points to the miraculous occurrence during the Prophet's migration. As they took refuge in a cave at Sawr, a spider quickly spun its web on the entrance of the cave. The pursuers of the Prophet were fooled by the web and did not even bother to check out the inside of cave. It is interesting that the verse initially talks about the flimsiness of the nest, and at the end it mentions, "if they only knew." The reason for this conclusion is that the flimsiness of spider nests is common knowledge; therefore, the verse must have another important meaning. Hence, the verse could also be indication the following notion, "if the nonbelievers realized how blind they were to the truth since and that they were even deceived by a spider's web, they would not have attempted to assassinate the Prophet."

---

An artist who paints two vases would wish that both paintings be equally beautiful. Then why did God create human beings with so many physical and physiological differences?

a.  Human beings are not copies of a single model; rather they are all inimitable designs of the truth that originates and manifests from divine names. A realist artist will paint the snake as a snake and a deer as a deer. Obviously, he/she would not paint a deer so that it appears as a snake. The artist should also paint the broken vase as it is. Hence, when he/she paints beautiful scenery with a variety of flowers, he/she does not exclude the caves or rocks from the masterpiece. Just as the example, God's beautiful names and supremacy manifest in many different ways. God has many divine names. These names manifest in many different forms, levels, and ranks.

For example, a king has many different titles, such as the king, the commander in chief, the Caliph, the judge, and so on. All of these titles manifest themselves on different occasions and in different circumstances. In law, he is the just ruler; in military terms, he is the high commander; and in guidance, he is the great Caliph. Although, they are all different titles and attributes, they are also interconnected. For instance, the existence of a police force is necessary so that the judge can perform his duty in a court of law. Just as the divine name *Muhyi* creates life, *Razzaq* provides sustenance. The name *Musawwir* fashions; the name *Muzayyin* decorates; and divine names like *Adl* and *Mukaddir* enable precision, fairness, and measurement.

Moreover, each divine name manifests at various ranks and levels. Let us take a look at the name Commander-in-Chief. It manifests on many ranks such as sergeants, captains, majors, generals, and admirals. So does the name *Muhyi* which manifests on all living organisms from a single-celled organism to human beings. The combination of many Divine Names produces countless living organisms and human beings of different appearances and character. There are millions of automobiles in the world and none of them have the same number plate. Even a single digit or a letter makes a huge difference. Indeed, the abilities, finger prints, and identity of no human being is a carbon of another.

b. Human beings are gifted with freewill, and they face trials within their own conditions. The rich, the poor, the healthy, and the disabled are put through different trials and tests. Therefore, they can obtain ranks that vary from the size of an atom to the size of a galaxy (Those who have mental disability and children are not held accountable).

c. This incredible diversity and variety cannot be coincidental. Out of the billions of human beings on earth, a minority in number are born without limbs or missing organs. If we were the products of an evolutionary accident, it would have been extremely uncommon to find a perfect human being. Whereas all living organisms possess complex bodies that suggest they are the product of an amazing designer. This means there is divine wisdom in some unusual cases of birth defects.

---

Thousands of chemical activities taking place within a single cell in a short time show that blind chance is impossible. On the other hand, it is claimed that certain inexplicable occurrences in the universe have divine reasons and wisdom. Can you enlighten us on this?

a. The Almighty is manifesting His omnipotence by doing things the way He wills. As some philosophers suggest, He is not obligated to act but He acts as He wills.

b. We are constantly reminded of the fact that human beings are feeble beings and that we need God at all times. This means that we need to beseech and

take refuge in God in all situations. Certain difficulties are given to certain people so that we are
reminded and warned to refrain from arrogance
and conceit. The comprehension of this important
issue will enable us to realize that we are His creation, and therefore his servants.

c. It is said that things are known by their opposites. If
   darkness did not exist, we would not have appreciated light; if sickness did not exist, we would not
   have appreciated health; if blindness did not exist,
   we would not have appreciated vision; if mental dis-
   orders did not exist, we would not have appreciated
   sanity. These deficiencies and disabilities are placed
   before us, so that we display gratitude for our well-
   being. The preciousness of the divine gifts is not
   detected because of the unchanging laws. Sunlight
   is no less of a great gift than rain. However, we fail
   to thank God for giving it to us because of the scientific knowledge we possess in relation to times of
   sunrise and sunset. Whereas, we believe that rain is
   mercy, and we often pray for it. The reason for this
   is rain was not attached to a regular law.

---

**We understand the divine wisdom in the creation of
people with disabilities, nevertheless, is it fair to them?**

The creation of people with disabilities is neither unfair
nor is it an act of injustice because injustice originates
from deprivation of rights. If someone took something

away from us that rightfully belonged to us, this would be injustice. However, all matter belongs to God, and he uses it as He wills. For example, a wealthy person walks into a gathering of the poor and begins to distribute money. He hands out different amounts of money to those at the gathering. Let us say, he gives one hundred dollars to one person and five hundred to another. Now, does the person who received a hundred dollars have the right to complain and say, "Why have you given me only a hundred?" The answer is no. Simply because the wealth belongs to the distributor, and the receivers should be grateful regardless of the amount they were granted.

The Almighty has created us out of nothing. He could have left us in the lower steps of the ladder of the biological species. For instance, we could have been created as a plant or a worm. Not only were we created as human beings, but we were also decorated with precious properties such as intelligence, self-awareness, emotions, and conscience. After receiving such invaluable gifts, no one has the right to be ungrateful due to certain physical disadvantages they may have.

———◈———

We acknowledge the fact that there is no injustice in the creation of disability, but how can we relate this to God's infinite compassion and mercy?

Having faith in afterlife death will solve this. The existence of an afterlife death can be proven with thousands of pieces of evidences. Therefore, those who were created with disabilities on earth will be generously rewarded for their patience. For example, the blind will be given the opportunity to observe Paradise from their graves. There are many things we observe on earth which provides pleasure for our eyes. The blind are deprived of this pleasure. Perhaps, in the afterlife, there will be many incredible things that only the blind will observe. When we compare a life of 60 to 80 years to eternity, we will realize that they are much more blessed than us. The only condition is that they have to be believers.

### Some people ask: if God does not need anything, why did He create the universe?

Creating does not come from necessity. Why would a supreme being, who has the power to create out of nothingness, feel a need? For example, helping the needy, the orphans, and those who are in poverty is a display of compassion, not a need. If this is the case for human beings, then how could we assume that God would need anything? Need originates from deficiency, and this cannot be associated to God. There is also the fact that He is the creator. How could He be a creator if He did not create?

### Why did God create the Angels?

a.  God did not create the angels because He needed them. Everything in the universe functions under the principle of cause and effect. This is God's will. In a large corporation, orders are given from the top, and they are conveyed to the smaller departments and branches. Just as the example, the eternal Sultan has officers and servants. However, they are not implementers. Therefore, they cannot be His partners in ruling. They are His message bearers. They proclaim and declare the Sultan's greatness and His magnificent acts and works. They are also observers of the Almighty's works, art, and power. Their obedience and gratitude can be considered as a form of worship.

Certainly, angels were created as "veils." They are the representatives of the Divine Decree and wise observers of creation.

From an atom to immense galaxies, everything recites the divine names of God and praises Him. The praise and worship of beings that do not possess intelligence or self-awareness are presented to God through the angels.

b. Angels are the only beings that perform their worship in total purity, without errors and hesitation.

c. They are also manifestations of God's divine name *Samad* (God does not need sustenance). Angels also do not need sustenance, and they have no gender.

---

### In the Qur'an, why does God use terms like 'Us' or 'We'?

a. The Qur'an is a divine book that rejects polytheism and emphasizes the existence of One Powerful God who creates everything with the infinite power of *Qahhar*. This is the mission and objective of the Qur'an. The terms used above should not be taken out of context.

b. In the structure of many languages, the term 'you' is used in the plural form to indicate respect. Likewise, the term "we" can be used instead of "I" as an expression of greatness.

When we analyze the Qur'anic scripture, we see that when the Qur'an refers to one individual, it uses the term "I." However, when the issue is a general one, the term 'We' is used. For example, in the following verse God speaks to Moses in an individualized manner: *Surely it is I, I am God; there is no deity save Me. So worship Me, and establish the Prayer in conformity with its conditions for remembrance of Me (Taha 20:14).* In this verse God Almighty is talking about Himself and uses the term "I." He wants His servants to believe only in Him and worship only Him.

However, in cases where He mentions creation or the revelation of the Qur'an, the act is generalized by the inclusion of all Divine Names. For example: *Indeed it is We, We Who send down the Reminder in parts, and it is indeed We Who are its Guardian (Hijr 15:9).* And in the following verses:

> *Have you considered the semen that you emit? Is it you who create it, or are We the Creator?* (Waqia 56:58-59).

They say that existence cannot appear from nonexistence, and it cannot be converted into nothingness.

a. This claim can only be valid for the creation not God. As human beings, our physical capabilities are limited by physical laws; therefore, we cannot create matter out of nothing, and we cannot send matter into nonexistence. People who come up with such arguments are using their own physical being as a model to make a comparison to the Supreme Being. Hence, this takes them to a dead-end. The reason for this is they wish to believe that matter, space, and time are eternal; however, this notion contradicts the second law of thermodynamics. Physical laws suggest that the universe is constantly losing energy and heading towards a thermo-equilibrium. Hence, all matter is heading towards an energetic death. This is called 'the thermodynamic apocalypse'.

This proves that matter is not eternal. This physical model also indicates that the end of the universe is inevitable. So the materialistic notion of 'eternal matter' has been refuted by physics. This means that matter and space-time were created.

b. Energy could only be converted to matter in the physical world; therefore, the claim that energy existed prior to matter is illogical.

c. Matter is made up of certain properties such as energy, heat, dimensions, motion, and so on. These properties were created after the creation of matter. The creation of motion occurred after immobility, cold was created after heat, and darkness was created after light. We know that immobility existed before motion. This means that immobility is not an eternal property because if it were, it would not have been replaced by motion. Eternal and infinite properties cannot be sent into nonexistence.

Just as the properties described above, matter also has a fundamental property. Even this fundamental property was created. The reason for this is matter cannot exist in the absence of the other essential properties. In conclusion, matter is not eternal.

The Almighty God performs the act of creation in two different ways:

1. He creates matter out of nothing and creates everything that is necessary for its continuity.

2. He designs and develops. Using His infinite wisdom to manifest His Divine Names, He uses the elements of the universe to develop and construct many different entities and living beings. Through the Divine Name, *Razzaq*, He gives sustenance to His creatures, sending atoms and particles to take on various duties and serve as nutrients. Creating out of nothing is one of His most basic laws and acts. Certainly, a creator that fashions thousands of different species that possess various qualities and

complex biological structures each spring no doubt possesses the ability to create out of nothing. Arguments put forward against this would be considered as illogical and unscientific. As human beings, we observe some of God's creation with our very eyes; however, there are things that can only be seen through reasoning. Unfortunately, we have nothing to say to those whose reasoning is limited to their eyesight.

———•⧝•———

Prophet Muhammad, peace and blessings be upon him, was the most beloved servant of God, yet his tooth was broken at a battle. Why did God allow this?

a. The noble Messenger of God is the perfect guide and a complete role-model for humanity in all of life's issues and matters. Therefore, all of his acts and physical performances could not be supernormal. If he were superhuman in every aspect, then he could not have been a perfect guide to us. For this reason, he took cover during battles, he wore armor, he felt the cold and pain, and his tooth was broken. It was imperative that he demonstrated the prayer under the difficult conditions of war so that we could learn this obligatory worship that was prescribed by the Qur'an, as it should be performed in all circumstances.

b. We have to remember that this world is a realm of assessment hence even the Prophet's patience is being tested here. With his extraordinary character that does not curse anyone, and unique compassion and self-sacrifice, he is teaching his followers perfect manners even on the battle fields. This indicates that the most important issue in life is saving the faith of human beings. We see this even on occasions where his feet were covered in blood and his tooth was broken. He continued to beseech mercy upon those who wished to harm him.

c. There is also the issue of atheism. In order to survive, atheism needs some type of support, because we live in a realm of assessment. If they had no argument points, they could not have survived resting on imaginary pillars. These types of occurrences are necessities of this grand test, and they emerge from the manifestations of Divine Grace (Jamal), and the manifestations of Divine Majesty (Jalal).

---

**Why do innocent people suffer during natural disasters, such as earthquakes?**

Natural disasters:

a. They purify people of their spiritual sins.

b. They promote the ranks of innocent people, saints, and martyrs.

In such catastrophes, children are the most innocent, if they were exempt, then the mystery of the test would be broken. For example, if a falling wall defied gravity and stopped half way in the air to protect the children, then this would have compelled all atheists to accept God. As a result, there would be no difference between Abu Jahl and Abu Bakr. Whereas, faith is a matter of choice. Doors are opened to intelligence, but no one is forced to enter. This way, the difference between the righteous and the rebel is established. It is common knowledge that answers are not given prior to or during the test. Hence, these kinds of occurrences act as veil so that those with pure faith and insight could be separated from the others. Otherwise, the opportunity to attain the highest rank of humanity would diminish.

---

**Earthquakes occur by the will of God. Whereas, non-believers claim that they are caused by natural forces. What is the role of God's Will in natural phenomena?**

In Surah Zilzal of the Holy Qur'an, God states:

> *"When the earth quakes with a violent quaking destined for it; And the earth yields up its burdens; And human cries out, "What is the matter with it?" –On that day, it will recount all its tidings, As your Lord has inspired it to do so."*

Each year, the earth goes through many geological and biological changes. Scientists tell us that millions of new species appear on earth each year. If we imagine each new species as a colorful string of wool, then in our mind, we would have a picture of the earth wearing new colorful and living clothes each year. Tulips, roses, reptiles, and flies can all be considered as amazing decorations of the earth. Out of millions of species, let us take the fly, for example. It is quite obvious that even the wings of a fly cannot be considered as a product of chance or accident. The reason for this is that from an engineering and design point of view, the wing structure of the fly is more complex than that of an aircraft.

When we consider the reality that even the wings of a fly is designed with complexity and magnificent know-how, then we would have to comprehend that the earth, which acts as a cradle for life, cannot be left to randomness. Small or large, every occurrence and motion on earth is monitored and controlled by the Almighty. An important part of the earth's dress is the living organism called the human being. This being is made up of one hundred trillion living cells with each cell containing over one million proteins and each protein containing thousands of amino acids. How can a being with such amazing complexity originate from randomness when we admit that even a simple protein chain cannot form by an accident? This means that the eternal power and knowledge of the Omnipotent God is involved in all occurrences that take place in the universe, including the earthquakes.

However, we have to remember, this is a place of testing and God has created a reason or a cause for every natural occurrence in the universe. Every thirty-three meters, we dig towards the center of the earth, and the temperature rises a degree. The center of the earth is extremely hot. This is why various levels of the magma are made up of molten metals and minerals. Perhaps God uses a chemical reaction as a cause to create earthquakes.

For example, a man shoots another person. If homicide detectives who are investigating the murder do not take the killer's involvement into consideration and say that the pistol killed the victim, they would be violating the rights of the victim. Just as the example, the Almighty explodes the earthquake like a bomb. He reminds rebellious souls of His power. Those innocent people who lose their lives during the disaster become martyrs. God considers their lost possessions as alms. The sinners become purified of their sins. In this case, if we neglected the real doer and concentrated only on the physical evidence, no one would derive a lesson from the disaster; people would be pushed into depression and despair by assuming that lives were lost for no reason. Such understanding would transform humanity into helpless beings who are deprived of consolation.

**Why do you correlate everything to divine wisdom and encourage people to derive a lesson from all happenings?**

When you analyze and observe this temporary guesthouse we call earth, you will see that nothing is out of order or purposeless. Then, how could a human being be without a cause or purpose?

> If disasters happen for a reason, perhaps to warn people,
> then why don't they strike nonbelievers particularly?

Disasters might strike anyone. They might even strike
believers more frequently, since the wrongdoings of believers are partially punished in this world through disasters.
However, significant crimes are referred to higher courts.
Therefore, the bigger crime of rebellion will be dealt with
on the Day of Judgment.

———•◦∞◦•———

> At the conclusion of Surah Luqman the five unknowns
> are mentioned (Mughayyabat al-Hamsa). Included in
> the five unknowns are the time of rain and the situation
> of the embryo in the mother's womb. These days, such
> things seem to be known. Weather stations can predict
> the time of rain and medical scientists can detect many
> things about the embryo, for example, they can estab-
> lish if the baby is going to be male or female. How
> could we explain this?

First of all we have to explain the meaning of *ghayb*—the
unseen, or anything beyond our knowledge and percep-
tion. In Qur'anic terms, *ghayb* is interpreted as things that
have not yet materialized. This means they have not come
to existence in the physical realm. The predictions made
by weather bureaus regarding the time of rain cannot be
considered as news from the *ghayb*. The reason for this is
the physical signs of rain have already materialized and
predictions are made according to these indications. Even
some people who have rheumatic fever can sense the
arrival of rain as pain in their legs. The air gets humid

before the rain, and humidity causes pain in their legs, but this is obviously a physical sign. Sensing the rain is also observed in certain animals.

This means prior to materialization there are certain indications which may be detected by scientific means or through natural senses. Weather bureaus take advantage of these scientific indications to make their predictions. It should be also noted that sometimes they can make errors in their calculations and fail in their predictions.

On the other hand, only God has knowledge of the rain that has not yet materialized. For example, can anyone predict when rain will fall next year?

Unlike sunrise, rain does not follow a certain schedule. It develops from the mercy of God and falls with His will. Natural occurrences such as sunrise and sunset follow a certain physical schedule, and for this reason God's power is veiled; hence, people fail to display gratitude. Since natural occurrences such as sunrise is a regular thing, human beings do not realize its significance for life. On the other hand, when rains do not come, people look for solutions such as performing prayers.

In relation to the embryo, the verse states, …*He alone knows what is in the wombs* (Luqman 31:34). This verse cannot be limited to gender prediction. God's knowledge about the developing embryo may be listed as: the child's destiny, character, special talents and abilities, the life he/s would encounter in the future, and psychological development. These and many other unique features can only be known by God.

---◦◦◦◦◦---

*"Until, when he reached the setting-place of the sun, he saw it setting in a spring of hot and black muddy water"* (Kahf 18:86). The verse suggests that Zulqarnayn's sun set in hot spring water. How could the sun which is more than a million times larger than the earth set in a river?

Sometimes, Qur'anic verses describe occurrences using metaphorical or allegorical methods so that everyone has a share according to their level of understanding. The verse means that Zulqarnayn marched a long way toward the west and went as far as the point where he (probably) saw a sea or ocean, appearing like a spring. The description of the sea or ocean as a spring of hot and black muddy water suggests that he had reached that point in the hottest days of summer when vaporization was at its greatest. Thus, it can be suggested that Zulqarnayn must have traveled towards the West of Africa during summer and reached the Atlantic coast.

The aim of the verse is not to say that the sun is smaller than the ocean. On the contrary, it mentions Zulqarnayn's observation of the sunset while it touches upon certain realities. For example, in a poetic way we may describe our journey in such manner by stating: *"As I traveled through foreign lands, one after another mountains stood on my path until I reached the coast one evening to watch the sun set in the sea, as if it was sinking into a bowl of red liquid."* As we use this literature, we are aware of the astronomical fact that the sun could not fit into the ocean. It is simply an analogical description.

However, this verse also has a concealed scientific indication. *"When he reached the setting of the sun, he found it set in a spring of hot water"* If we use the Mecca meridian, where the Qur'anic verse was revealed, as our beginning point, the sun sets 90% towards the West meridian. This is the Sargasso Sea, the region where the Gulfstream that warms the European coastline begins to flow.

We have to look also at the issue from the Qur'an's perspective, a divine book that observes the entire universe. The Qur'an does not only see the issue from Zulqarnayn's perspective. Since it is a book that came from the heavens, sometimes it refers to earth as a palace, a small area, or a cradle, and at times it refers to it as a page. The Qur'anic concept of time is much different from ours. Sometimes it talks about a day that lasts a thousand years compared to our time. Sometimes, it reminds us that a Qur'anic day is equivalent to fifty thousand years of our time.

For this reason, it is quite rational for the Qur'an to talk about the setting of the sun into the Atlantic Ocean because according to this divine book, the sun is a tiny object that plays the role of a light globe in our solar system. Moreover, from a distance, a lake could be seen as a small pool of water. Accordingly, the sun or the ocean may be observed as tiny bodies by heavenly eyes.

In Surah Ikhlas, God is described as being Al-Samad. Al-Samad means that everything needs Him but He needs nothing. It is obvious that God does not need our prayers and worship, then why does He insist on our worship?

Just as our stomach and body needs food and nutrition, our soul and emotions need worship. Moreover, human beings were sent to earth for a purpose of being tested. Therefore, they were equipped with certain detrimental feelings and emotions so that they could show patience as they struggle with their carnal souls and the whispers of Satan. They can only reach their goal of perfection through such significant struggle. For this reason, throughout their lives, human beings encounter metaphysical problems and spiritual illnesses. Daily prayers are the best medicine and a remedy for curing these illnesses. For example, a patient visits the local doctor. The doctor writes a prescription for the illness and reminds the patient over and over again about how the medicine should be taken. How logical would it be if the patient asks the doctor, "Why are you relentlessly insisting that I use this medicine, do you have need for this?" A question like this would be quite irrational because it is the patient that needs the medicine, not the doctor.

---

Some philosophers argue that all living beings exist to serve themselves and they belong only to this planet. This is contrary to scientific research which suggests that everything exists for a reason and that there is no squander in the universe. This brings a question to our minds; human beings are gifted with amazing physical and spiritual abilities. Yet they live approximately 70-80 years. Some even die before reaching the age of puberty. Is this not a waste? There are insects with incredible body structures and design. Yet they live no more than an hour. How could we explain such thing?

Philosophers do not observe life through the golden lens of the Holy Qur'an; hence, their perspectives are inadequate. Everything exists with an objective and purpose. The purpose of their being is not restricted to this world only. This is why the argument of squander or waste is not valid. Qur'anic interpretations have explained these purposes under three main headings:

1. Purpose concerning the creator: all creatures present themselves before their Maker as if they were participating in an enormous parade. This manifestation is adequate even if it occurs for a brief moment.

2. God's magnificent works of art is being exhibited before intelligent beings so that they could read them like a book or a poem and examine their meanings.

3. The purpose concerns the creature itself. This involves insignificant things such as living, indulgence, and comfort.

Since philosophy is only concerned with the third point, it does not understand the meaning of existence. Let us remember that not all seeds become trees and not all eggs hatch. Some were created so that others could consume them. Even this is enough to prove that there is no waste in creation. According to the first point, it is obvious that God has knowledge about the potential of the seeds and eggs that would become trees or birds. This means there is divine wisdom in serving them as sustenance to other creatures; hence, there is also divine wisdom in the prevention of further development. This also forms an ecological balance in the environment. For example, if all larvae were to become flies, earth would have been covered with flies within a short period of two years. If millions of fish eggs were not consumed by other animals, the fish population would have grown out of control and there would be no other creature left in the oceans.

This means that philosophy could only see one percent of the purpose and fails to detect the other ninety-nine percent. For example, there are many different purposes in military training, such as establishing law and order, protecting the borders of the nation, combating the enemy, building a powerful nation and so on... How rational would it be to claim that soldiers are necessary only for keeping the law and order, so we should keep the gendarme and abolish rest of the army? Obviously, this is not the only purpose of the army and the other services cannot be considered as useless extras.

You have explained that all creatures have a purpose to exist. In the Qur'anic translations are there any other

reasons for the creation of living beings that exist only
for a short period of time?

Indeed there are and let us take a look at some of these
reasons:

a. Living beings are like the metallic alphabet that the
   printers use in their offset machines. Once all the
   pages of a book are completed, these metallic letters are not dumped into the rubbish bin. The
   essential material is reused for printing new books.
   Just as the example, every single deed of ours is
   recorded by the angels and sent to the metaphysical
   worlds, such as the Alam al-Mithal (the World of
   Representations or Ideal Forms), and Lahw al-
   Mahfuz (The Supreme Ever-Preserved Tablet). This
   is followed by new recordings and meanings sent
   after a short period of time. The living beings
   recorded previously have completed their mission
   and have moved on to make way for new manifestations and meanings.

b. All recordings are sent to angels and other spirituals
   beings that analyze and scrutinize the data. Occurrences are examined according to the manifestations of the divine Names.

c. According to a saying of the Prophet that describes
   the world as a cultivation ground for the afterlife,
   not only the deeds of human beings are sent to the
   Divine Courts, but the actions and behaviors of all
   animals are also sent there. For example, even if we

do not possess the means to travel to Africa, we could obtain information about the life styles of the people, plants, and animals by viewing a documentary about this continent. Who could resist watching everything that had occurred in history, since the time of Prophet Adam? Moreover, would we not prefer to view a recording of our own lives?

The Holy Qur'an (Saffat 37:44) explains that the obedient servants of God will enjoy Paradise sitting on thrones, face to face. The verse also indicates that all conversations and occurrences that take place on earth can be found and viewed in Paradise. Since, the curtain of metaphysics will be raised there, everything will be observed clearly with their divine reasons and manifestations of the Divine Names. Everything that occurs during spring is recorded. Seasons and the lifespan of all creatures (including the universe in its entirety) are recorded and shall be presented like embroidery decorated with divine manifestations and power.

d. For example, human beings consume a variety of fruits that eventually dissolve and diminish in the digestive system. However, in addition to the mouth, tongue, and the stomach, all the living cells benefit from it. Moreover, it helps the body sustain itself and continue living. All of these various vegetables and fruits transform from plant life and rise to the rank of human life. Even these simple life forms attain a higher level of temporary lives in the human body. Each scene and episode of these transformations is also recorded by the angels.

e. Imagine a magnificent machine that functions in a large factory. Many basic substances are fed into this machine. Apparently, these elements burn away and become destroyed, but their destruction produces many significant chemicals and compounds. Moreover, their fiery destruction produces power and energy that fuels the machines that in turn produce products, like clothes and food. This means that many significant products are obtained with the burning of a simple substance. So a simple substance disappears, but it gives rise to many wonderful products.

Similarly, the Almighty God grants motion to the enormous factory of the universe. He uses the temporary bodies of existence as seeds for eternal bodies. He uses everything as a means for His divine purpose; they become ink for His pen that records destiny and strings that are used as ornaments in His divine embroidery. He brings the universe into action, and it silently recites and writes His verses.

f. Every soul is used as a model that He dresses with new clothes each year. From a single book, the Almighty produces thousands of books, and the storyline changes constantly.

g. In this limited earth, God constantly changes His designs and artwork to produce new and original products and gifts. If there was no motion in atoms and no transformation in creatures, the fruits that we pick would not be replaced by new ones each year.

h. All the products of the afterlife and divine destiny are produced and decorated in this life and realm. A world that could be considered a small pond needs to work constantly to produce the spiritual products that would eventually fill the realm of the afterlife which resembles an immense ocean. As a world of sights makes its way towards the realm of hereafter, there is no need for replicas. For this reason, the Almighty God renews His products constantly.

———◈◈◈———

We frequently pray to our Lord and ask for many things, yet most of our prayers are not answered. Whereas, God states: *"Pray to me and I will answer you"* (Mu'min 40:60). Since the verse addresses all of humanity, why doesn't God answer some of our prayers?

Answering and accepting are different things. Every prayer is answered but acceptance and God's endowment for what is asked depends on divine wisdom. For example, a patient visits the doctor. The doctor then asks the patient what s/he wants. The patient may sometimes say: "Give me this medicine". The doctor will not write the prescription before examining the patient. Following the examination, if the requested medicine is beneficial, it will be prescribed. However, if there is something else that would be more beneficial to the patient, the doctor will prescribe that particular medicine.

The Almighty God is present everywhere and at all times; thus, He answers all prayers. He removes the frightening sense of loneliness from the hearts of His servants. However, using divine wisdom, He bestows what is needed, not what is requested. Sometimes, He gives what is asked and sometimes He gives what is better. For example, one may ask for a baby boy, but God may give him a baby girl, like Mary the mother of Jesus. Obviously, a mother of a prophet is more blessed than a baby boy. However, on some occasions He may not bestow a child at all.

We have to remember that prayers are a type of worship. Their rewards will be given in the hereafter.

---

**If prayers are rewarded in the hereafter, then why do we perform a prayer for rain?**

Worldly objectives designate the time of certain prayers. They are not the goal. The prayer for rain is a type of worship. Its time is designated by drought. This prayer is not offered for the sole purpose of rain. If this was the only goal, it would not be accepted because it would be lacking the necessary element of sincerity.

### So what is the purpose of the prayers performed during solar and lunar eclipses?

Just as sunset indicates the time of the Maghrib (evening) prayer,a solar or lunar eclipse indicates the time of the relevant (Kusuf and Khusuf) prayers. The divine wisdom is explained in the Qur'an:

> *We have made the night and the day two signs (manifesting the truth of God's Power, Knowledge, and absolute sovereignty, and His grace on you). We have obscured the sign of the night (made it dark), and We have made the sign of the day illuminating (therefore, a means for you) to see, that you may seek bounty from your Lord and that you may know the computation of (time) the years and the reckoning* (Isra 17:12).

The astronomical events such as the solar and lunar eclipses are manifestations of the Divine power. This is why God prescribes His servants to offer prayers during their occurrences. These prayers are not performed so that the moon or the sun is released from captivity. This is quite obvious because astronomers have detailed information about the duration of both eclipses.

Times of disaster, calamity, catastrophe, and misfortune also indicate the time of certain types of prayer and worship. In such unfortunate times, human beings realize their weaknesses and helplessness and, therefore, turn to their creator and take refuge in His mercy and compassion. Even if the problem does not diminish contrary to persistent prayers, one should not say, "My prayers were not answered."Instead, one should say, "The time of acceptance has not arrived yet." This prayer would only be completed when the Almighty God removes the burden or the problem with His eternal mercy and compassion.

This means prayer is a form of servanthood. And authentic servanthood is performed only for the sake of God. Therefore, we have to display our weaknesses and seek refuge in Him through our prayers. However, we must leave the result up to God and trust His decision. We should never criticize His mercy and question His verdict.

---

In the Surah Nur (24:41) God informs us: "Do you not see that all that is in the heavens and the earth, and the birds flying in patterned ranks with wings spread out glorify God. Each knows the way of its prayer and glorification. God has full knowledge of all that they do." According to the verse, there are different types and forms of prayers. How can we classify them?

Prayers can be categorized in three main groups:

The first type of prayer is made through the language of ability and capability. All seeds and kernels pray by using this language. It is through this prayer that small realities transform into huge trees that give fruits.

Causes can also be considered as this type of prayer. For example: water, heat, light, and earth unite around the seed and pray, "Oh Lord! Transform this seed into a tree." Otherwise, it would be quite illogical to assume that these unintelligent properties possess the ability to create a tree. Some people claim that growing and nurturing healthy plants depends on the time of germination and fertilization; therefore, it has nothing to do with metaphysics. Nothing could be further than the truth because all causes unite through a powerful prayer. This is evident because even if we follow all the procedures with perfect timing, sometimes we do not get results. For instance, there are trees that give fruits throughout the year, and then for no apparent reason, they give nothing the following year. These fruits are coming from the treasures of the eternal mercy; hence, they are created through the language of prayers.

The Second type of prayer is the prayer made through the needs of natural disposition. All living beings pray to their All-Generous Lord to obtain their indispensable needs which are beyond their reach and capability. These needs, necessary to sustain life, are provided from a mysterious source with amazing timing. The acceptance of a prayer is evident because the necessities and provisions provided by God are beyond the reach of all living beings.

The third type of prayer is performed by intelligent beings to obtain their countless needs. This category can also be divided into four groups:

a. Prayers of those who are in trouble or danger. In Surah Naml (27:62), God reminds us that it is) *He Who answers the helpless one in distress when he prays to Him, and removes the affliction from him...* All intelligent beings surrender, submit, and beseech the aid of a mysterious power when they are in great distress or danger. They all seek refuge in Him and plead for salvation.

b. A prayer made for fundamental needs; We all need sustenance, and God provides for us.

c. A prayer that befits the language of ability; e.g. an apple seed wishes to grow into an apple tree.

d. A prayer made with the purity and genuineness of the heart.

Most of the time, these four types of prayers are acceptable. Prayers play the greatest role in success, great discoveries, and achievements accomplished by human beings. This means that all the great scientific and technological achievements of today's civilization are answers to prayers made in the form of insistent and consistent work and effort displayed by human beings. They are gifts and blessings bestowed by the Almighty. These prayers were not offered through the tongue but through the language of ability and capability. On most occasions, these types of prayers are answered.

However, there is an important issue that we should not overlook here. When Prophet Suleyman brought the throne of Queen of Sheba from Yemen, he said: *"This is by the Grace of my Lord!- to test me whether I am grateful or ungrateful! And if any is grateful, truly his gratitude is (gain) for his own soul; but if any is ungrateful, truly my Lord is Free of all Needs, Supreme in Honor!" (Surah Naml: 40)*. This means that the technological wonders bestowed upon us through prayers should be used responsibly and in a way that it would please God. Using them for evil or indecency would mean an act of ingratitude.

There is also another form of prayer that consists of two parts:

a. Performed through action: For example, plowing the soil can be considered as knocking on the door of the treasures of divine mercy. This prayer will be answered on most occasions if it is performed by obeying the laws of physics (natural causes). The reason for this is one would be obeying the physical laws that have been created and implemented by God.

b. Performed through language: This prayer is offered by the tongue or the heart. The most important essential of this prayer is that the person who performs it must be in the realization of the infinite Power Who possesses the knowledge to hear everything in the person's heart, and has the power to fulfill all requests made by his helpless, weak servants who stand before Him. In the universe, there is no bigger and better support for mankind.

---

**What would you say about all the evil and ugly occurrences that take place in the universe?**

Liberty entails error and mistakes. Freedom would have no meaning in an environment where the right to choose between right and wrong is removed. Freewill prevails between obedience and rebellion. God has the power to make obedient, blessed souls out of all of us. However, this would mean oppression into submission; freedom would be removed. So in order to achieve true liberty, the formation of evil has to be tolerated.

According to this, a nonbiased view and compassionate conscience will realize that beauty, perfection, and blessedness are the main objectives of existence and evil is an ugly exception. For example, health is the foundation of life but illness is an exception. If we compare health to illness, what portion of life consists of health and what portion is affected by illnesses? All natural disasters such as earthquakes, hurricanes and tsunamis can be regarded as a few minutes compared to the millions of years that the earth has existed. So, the casualties caused by disasters and wars can be considered as temporary cramps compared to history of mankind.

Moreover, matter is identified by its opposite component. It is through this mixture and diversity that many realities are observed. For example, beauty is recognized through ugliness, and light is realized through darkness. In addition, the level of such properties can only be detected through the involvement of their opposites.

We also believe that everything has a blessing attached to it. For instance, illnesses strengthen the immune system; problems and tribulations enhance patience and tolerance; volcanoes erupt to release the buildup of extreme pressure within the magma of the earth protecting the crust from more serious explosions. They also provide precious minerals. Through wars people come together around the table of truce to work out their differences and to look for solutions. Many important discoveries were made during wars, such as penicillin, atoms, rocket fuel, and jets. Some medicines are made from the toxic venom of snakes. Let us not forget that there are many types of good bacteria. Death may seem evil, but it is the only way that eternal life could be obtained. Just imagine if no one had died. The earth would be filled with billions of suffering old people. How could we have survived?

The evil that exists in the universe is like a shadow we see in paintings. As we look closer into the picture, we may think that there is an error or inaccuracy in the masterpiece. However, when we look at it from a distance, observing the entire picture, we realize the necessity of the shadows. We understand that the picture would not be complete without the shadows that play an important role in the beauty of the masterpiece.

As Imam Ghazali stated, "The bent appearance of the bow is the biggest evidence to its correctness because if it was straight, it would be useless for the arrow. Therefore, the deficiencies we observe in the universe point to perfection."

Indeed, if ailments did not exist, we would not appreciate health. Health is like the jewel in the crown. Unfortunately, we only realize its value when we lose it. Could we have cherished beauty if ugliness did not exist?

Another reason why problems, difficulties, and burdens exist is that they play a major role in unearthing the hidden treasures embedded in the souls of human beings.

We have to also remember that human story is not limited to this world. This story has many episodes. Death is not the last chapter; on the contrary, it is the very beginning. It would be unfair to pass judgment about an entire play by viewing only one part. Similarly, it would be unjust to criticize a book by reading a single chapter.

Blessings are from God, and evil comes from the carnal soul. Without doubt, God has created winds and storms. He has created rivers and oceans. Does a greedy captain who overloads his ship have the right to blame God when his ship sinks in bad weather? Anyone who has an ounce of commonsense would refrain from blaming the Creator for the evil that occurs on earth.

The reason for eternal punishment (hellfire):

Those condemned to eternal punishment for their sins will plead to God asking for a second chance to be returned to earth to perform good deeds. God replies in the Holy Qur'an:

> *...and if they were brought back to the world, they would revert to the very thing they were forbidden: indeed, they are just liars* (Anam 6:28).

This means that their sins were not restricted by time. On the contrary, if allowed they would have continued to sin for eternity. So, rebellion is an attribute of their carnal soul. It is not a temporary feeling of revolt limited by this world or a certain period of time. The following verses describe the character of these individuals quite explicitly:

*When an affliction befalls human, he calls upon his Lord turning to Him (in contrition); then when He bestows a favor upon him, he forgets for what he prayed to Him before, and sets up rivals to God, so that he (himself goes astray and) mislead (others) from His way. Say (to such a one): "Enjoy life in your unbelief for a while! You are for sure one of the companions of the Fire.* (Zumar 39:8)

*And if We let him taste ease and plenty after some hardship has visited him, he says: "Gone is all affliction from me!" Surely he is prone to vain exultation and self-glorifying* (Hud 11:10).

In another verse, God describes them as follows:

*The Day when God will raise them all from the dead, they will swear to Him as (now) they swear to you. They fancy that they will have some standing (through their oaths). Be aware: they are but liars.* (Mujadila 58:18).

Even on the great Day of Judgment, when everything is revealed and nothing could be concealed, they will appear before God and attempt to defend their carnal soul by lying and behaving in a dishonest manner.

In conclusion, we are not talking about sins and rebellion committed during a certain period of time. This is a rebellion that continues even after time has been abolished and the universe has come to an end. This is a soul that carries its evil towards eternity. For this reason, infinite evil deserves eternal punishment, and this is true justice.

> If a hundred people requested a hundred different things from a person, he could not comply. Whereas, millions of people continuously pray and ask for different things from God. Can you enlighten us on this issue?

First of all, it would be wrong to compare human beings who have limited power, knowledge, and freewill to the Almighty God. Moreover, we observe some incredible qualities and abilities even amongst His creation. This alone should be enough to give us some ideas about what God is capable of doing. For example, even a single air molecule has the ability to carry and convey all the radio and TV signals emitted by stations all over the world. This means that air molecules have the potential to carry and convey these signals without mixing them up. When we listen to our radio stations, we recognize the voices quite clearly. The molecules perform this duty efficiently and without any confusion. Whereas if we attempt to place two dots within a space that could hold only one dot, there will be a jumble. The jumble will be inevitable even if we use two different pens. On the other hand, millions of different frequencies and vibrations go through the air molecules without being jumbled. Let us not forget the fact that these molecules also transmit properties such as electricity, light, and heat and provide a service to all living organisms. All of these magnificent duties are performed without any errors and mix-ups. The air molecules also perform such duties as helping plant reproduction and fertilization. How can any act be difficult for God when a simple molecule He has created performs so many incredible duties?

---◦≪◦≫◦---

There are certain prayers and recitations prescribed by important scholars. However, not everyone benefits from reciting these prayers. Can you explain why?

Prayers and recitations should be regarded as different types of worship. They are the necessities of servanthood. They are performed with an intention to please God. Their benefits and rewards will be collected in the hereafter. Therefore, performing prayers with an expectation of a reward in this life will damage the essence of servanthood. If worldly objectives are excluded from the prayers, the Almighty God may grant some form of reward to the worshipper. Moreover, He may even grant extraordinary blessings to weak souls in order to strengthen their faith. These are the unique benefits emphasized by important scholars; however, they should not be the aim and objective of our prayers. It would be quite irrational to consume these eternal fruits in this temporary and transient world.

---◦≪◦≫◦---

According to the following verses no one should die of hunger. Whereas, some claim that there are people dying of hunger. How can we explain this?

*How many a living creature there is that does not carry its own provision (in store), but God provides for them, and indeed for you. He is the All-Hearing, the All-Knowing* (Ankabut 29:60).

*Surely God – it is He Who is the All-Providing, Lord of all might, and the All-Forceful.* (Dhariyat 51:58).

In reality, no one dies due to lack of sustenance. The reason for this is some of the sustenance sent by God is reserved in the bodies of living beings in the form of fat. Even living tissues have deposits of fat reserves. These reserves are used by living cells when fresh sustenance fails to arrive.

Those who allegedly die from starvation die before using these food reserves. This means their anatomy was not prepared for such emergencies. People who fast and eat their meals according to prophetic tradition have been known to go without food for long periods of time. The reason for this is their bodies have been prepared for such emergencies. Since, the time of the noble Prophet, the armies of Islam have proved this reality over and over again. The life styles of those who refrain from the temptations of the world are also great example of this.

In reality, people who purportedly die from starvation are the people who have regular eating habits. Although, habits such as smoking, drinking, and drugs are not necessities of life, some cannot do without them. There are those who come to the brink of death when they could not find these substances. Just as the example, those who make a habit out of eating too much resemble a drug addict. They develop fatal illnesses in times of scarcity and food shortage.

According to research, the fat reserves in living bodies can sustain life for forty days. In some unusual cases, this period may even extend to eighty days. This means that those who die before the forty day barrier do not really die from starvation. Perhaps, they die from illnesses formed by abandoning a habit. There is no such a thing as dying from starvation. Under normal circumstances the merciful name of Razzaq comes to the aid before the natural food reserves of the body runs out. He provides sustenance at most unexpected times from the breasts of animals and from the timber of trees.

Just think about a helpless baby in the mother's womb who does not possess even the power to move its lips. Its sustenance is provided miraculously through a tube in its tummy. Once the infant arrives to this world, all it needs to do is to move its mouth to suck out the miraculous liquid of life prepared in the mother's breasts in a most amazing way. The amount of milk is increased with each passing day, and its chemical composition is changed in accordance to the biological needs of the newborn. Initially, mother's milk contains traces of sugar and nourishments. However, its composition changes gradually. The amount of sugar and fat in the mother's milk increases with each passing day. This enables the baby's organs and cells to develop in a healthy way.

In relation to milk, we observe a unique display of compassion in kangaroos. Sometimes, mother kangaroos give birth whilst they are breast-feeding their previous newborns. Obviously, the newborn needs to feed on different milk than the six or seven month old young. In such situation, two types of milk begin to flow from the breasts of the mother. The newborn drinks from the less concentrated milk whilst the others drink from the thicker milk which contains more nourishment. Just as the example, the All-Compassionate Master manifests His mercy by providing living beings sustenance before the natural fat reserves in the body run out. He does not desert any of His creatures to death by starvation unless there are other evil factors involved. As we can observe there are some people in some communities suffering from severe shortage of food, but their suffering occurs mainly due to wrong economic or military policies, mismanagement, as well as abuse, neglect, and exploitation of the rich nations, depriving these people of sufficient food to ensure survival; poor health conditions also play a great role in such deaths.

---

How is it possible for Azrail, the angel of death, to collect all the souls simultaneously? It is also said that Azrail appears to everyone in a different way during the time of death. For example, to prophets he comes with a different face than to evildoers. Some see a beautiful face while others see a horrific figure. How is this possible?

One person can become many using variety of mirrors. The image reflected by the mirror can be different, and mirrors themselves can vary in shape and size. For example, human beings, the sun, angels, and words may have various reflections. Furthermore, properties such as water, air, time, spiritual beings, imagination, and thoughts can also be considered as different types of mirrors or reflections.

There are various types of reflections and images:

1. Reflection of solid matter: For example, if we stepped into a room with a thousand mirrors, we would see a thousand different images of ourselves. A single hand gesture displayed by us will be reflected in all the mirrors. However, our reflection in the mirror does not possess the properties of life. For instance, it is impossible for a person to have a conversation with his own or someone else's reflection.

2. Reflection of matter with properties of light: For example, the sun is reflected by all transparent objects, such as glass and water. However, it is not only the sun's image reflected in this case; the seven colors of the spectrum and heat also passes through. What we observe in the glass is only a mere reflection of the sun but with the properties mentioned above it would seem as if there was a tiny sun that existed within the glass. For instance, using the sunlight and a magnifying glass we could set fire to almost anything. If we hold a tilted mirror towards the sun and a dark room, the reflection of the sun would brighten the room.

This means that even though the sun is millions of kilometers away from all objects on earth, it is also quite close to everything. Indeed, we are quite a distance away from the sun, yet it strokes our heads with its rays and warms our bodies. As it engages with the ocean, it also shows itself in a single drop of water. One duty does not obstruct the other. The small does not obstruct the big, and the few do not obstruct the many. It affects many different objects at the same instant.

3. Reflection of illuminated souls: For example, the reflection of an angel is the same as itself. It is living and possesses the same properties as the original self. However, their manifestation varies depending on the ability of the mirror. They do not appear on all mirrors with their entire epitome. For instance, angel Gabriel appeared before the Prophet as a beautiful human being who reminded him of a *sahaba* named Dihya, but at the same instant, he was at a prostration position before God, with his grandeur appearance and astounding wing structure. At the same time, God knows, how many other locations he was at, conveying the divine decrees.

The saints who have attained the rank of *Abdali-yah* could also appear in many different locations at the same instant, because they have earned the qualities of *Nur* (divine light). Therefore, they could have conversations with many different people at

many different locations at the same instant. Azrail
(the angel of death) is also an angel, so he possesses
the qualities of divine light. For this reason, he
could appear in many places at the same time. One
of his duties will not get in the way the others. At
the same time, just as the mirror example given
above, when we step into a room that contains a
thousand mirrors, if all the mirrors have different
qualities such as different sizes, curves, and colors,
our reflection in all the mirrors would have a different appearance. Similarly, the angel of death manifests himself differently to the souls of human beings
who shape their spiritual mirrors with their own
deeds. At the time of death, if the individual is a
person who has a dark heart, the angel will appear
on it as a horrific creature of the dark. On the other
hand, to an innocent person, he will appear as a
most trustable friend who will collect the soul as
easy as removing a hair from butter.

---

According to a Hadith in Bukhari and Muslim, Prophet
Moses slapped the angel of death and gouged one of
his eyes out. Is this possible and if it really happened,
does the angel of death has only one eye now?

We should not compare angels to human beings. Angels
can appear in many different shapes and bodies. Azrail,
the angel of death, is the chief and general supervisor of
all the angels who collect souls at the time of death.

However, there is the question of whether Azrail collects all the souls himself or angels working under his command perform this duty. There are three different views in regards to this question. Let us analyze them one by one;

1. Azrail collects the souls of all living beings. Performing one duty does not hinder him from performing another, because he has the properties of the divine light. We have explained this in our previous question. According to this view, Azrail's reflection on the soul of Moses at the time of death was exclusive to Moses only. Therefore, it is not impossible for a great Prophet such as Moses to slap in fury his private reflection of the angel across the face. So, the gouging of the angel's eye should not be considered as illogical. The reason for this is it does not involve the very essence of Azrail but his mere reflection on the mirror of the soul. For example, if someone were to slap our reflection on the mirror, this would not cause any harm to us.

2. Great angels such as Gabriel, Mikhail, Israfil, and Azrail should be considered as general supervisors. From their own species, they have a large team under their command. These servants are tiny versions of these great angels. However, their manifestations are proportional to beings with whom they interact. For example, the angels that collect the souls of pious, righteous, obedient servants of God are different than the angels that collect the souls of

rebellious human beings. This is quite evident in the initial verses of Surah Naziat: *"By the (angels) who tear out (the souls of the wicked) with violence. By those who gently draw out (the souls of the blessed)."* According to this view, the angel that appeared before Moses was not Azrail himself but a body of entity that represented the angel of death. Therefore, it is quite possible for Moses to slap this angelic being across the face. The reason for this is that by nature Moses was a courageous individual who had a high position by the side of God. Perhaps, from the perspective of prophethood, such events occurred to due to a certain divine wisdom.

3. Prophet Muhammad states, "There are certain angels who possess forty-thousand heads and on each head there are forty-thousand mouths that have forty-thousand tongues which recite His divine Names." This Hadith may be interpreted as worship performed by angels is the most orderly, perfect, and collective form of submission. The Hadith also indicates that angels represent a countless number of creatures; therefore, their representation of the existence is enormous and extremely detailed. For example, an angel that has certain duties in the heavens above needs to possess a thousand heads in order to represent the stars and the galaxies. For instance, an almond tree that has forty branches that represents forty tongues and each branch has forty flowers with forty crests amazingly designed and decorated with magnificent colors. Obviously, an angel that repre-

sents this tree would be manifesting in accordance to the appearance of the tree.

Therefore, this view suggests that Azrail has a different face for each individual with whom he interacts. Imagine an enormous electric terminal that supplies electricity to an entire city. With a push of a button the electricity supplied to a certain house, region, or even the entire city can be cut off. If each light globe were connected to this huge terminal, they could even be turned off individually. Just as the example, angel Azrail has a connection with every soul in the universe. At the time of death, this connection is enabled and human beings experience a direct current between Azrail and themselves. Another example is the network system in computers. If a thousand computers are connected to a master computer, this master computer may and can switch off any or all of the computers connected to it.

The angel of death has the ability to connect into the frequencies of all living beings. Without doubt, he has also connected into the frequency of Moses. Therefore, it would be quite irrational to assume that Moses had slapped Azrail's very being or attempted to obstruct the angel from performing his duty. On the contrary, he stroked a face that wished to put a stop to his mission of Prophethood, which he wanted to continue. Since the face was only a reflection and there was no harm to Azrail himself, the incident is a possibility. Moreover, Moses is one of the great Prophets, and therefore God has permitted for such thing to occur.

**According to another Hadith the world stands on top of an ox and a fish. How could this be possible?**

In a Hadith transmitted by Ibn Abbas, they asked the Messenger of God, "What does the earth stand on?" He replied, "On top of a fish and an ox."

Some people, who took ancient Hebrew superstition as the basis for their interpretations have sidetracked the real meaning of this Hadith. Also, according to an ancient Hindu belief, the earth rests on the horns of a mother cow. As the great mother cow moves its head, the earth experiences series of earthquakes.

Now let us analyze this Hadith from an Islamic perspective:

Angels are representatives of physical laws and creatures that have no self-awareness. They are the presenters of prayers performed by intelligent beings and observers of God's magnificent work. Each rain drop is brought down to the earth's surface by an angel. The bearers of the Divine Throne are sometimes called the Ox, the Vulture, the Man, or some other title. These are in fact angels. Therefore the ox and fish mentioned in the Tradition in question could be referring to these angels. Otherwise, the placing of the Divine Throne and the earth on the back of an ox, an animal which is not self-sufficient, is opposed to the order of the universe. In addition, there is an angel appointed for every species of existence. This angel manages the affairs of that species. The angel is called by the name of the species for which it is responsible and appears with its form in the world of the angels. There is a saying of the Prophet reported by Imam Bukhari: "The sun goes up before the Divine Throne every evening, prostrates itself, and is given permission to return." The angel responsible for the sun is called "the Sun," and is in the shape of the sun. Obviously, it is not the sun that leaves the galaxy but the angel named Shams (sun) who makes this journey.

Just as some Qur'anic verses, Hadiths also contain metaphorical meanings. Unfortunately, when metaphoric explanations fall into the hands of ignorance instead of wisdom, the truth becomes diverted. For example, astronomers of the past drew a certain orbit of motion for the moon and suggested that the sun also followed a path through the astrological constellations. They believed that the orbital paths of the sun and the moon apparently crossed at certain point in space. At the crossing point, two curves with an angle of five degrees appeared. These two curves seemed like two snakes facing each other with their mouths opened. For this reason, they named the crossing points the head and the tail. When the moon was at the position of the head, the sun was at the tail, and the earth was in the middle, a lunar eclipse occurred. According to a metaphorical description, the moon was swallowed by the snake. However, later on, this astronomical expression was misinterpreted by ignorant people who truly believed that the moon was being swallowed by a gigantic space snake. The stories made up by these people were so fantastic that they even claimed the space snake was transparent hence the moon was still visible even after being swallowed by it.

The great angels named appropriately Ox and Fish also indicate an astronomical occurrence. Unfortunately, when they moved from the Prophet's mouth onto the tongues of ignorant people, they became a gigantic ox and a horrendous fish.

There are two important reasons as to why these angels were named Ox and Fish. The earth is made up of two important components, earth and water. The waters are ornamented by fish, and the land is processed by farming. Without doubt, farming rests on the shoulders of the ox. So, there is a metaphorical reason for the names given to these two angels.

1. Fish is the main sustenance of those who live in the coastal regions of the world. On the other hand, processing and cultivating the earth has been done through the ox for many centuries. For example, they say that "a nation stands on a pen and a sword." This means that a nation without military or scholars cannot survive. So like the nation analogy, it would be quite logical to argue that the earth stands on fish and an ox simply because the survival of humanity rests on fish and farm animals.

   We should also approach the issue from a historical point of view. Questions such as the ones above were put forward during a time when advancement in science was quite insignificant.

They could not have comprehended the issue in the way we do today, so they were given answers in accordance to their understanding. For example, the Qur'an answers a question put forward to the noble Prophet:

> *They ask you about the New Moons (Because of the Ramadan). Say: They are appointed times (markers) for the people (to determine time periods) and for the Pilgrimage (Baqara 2:189).*

The Qur'an answers the questions of those who wished to be informed about the essence of the moon and its motion. Throughout history, moon cycles have played a great role in the making of calendars. Of course, the moon's visibility depends on the position of the sun but such astronomical explanation would have been useless and incomprehensible to people of that era. The Qur'an provides the most appropriate explanation to people who had no knowledge of the gravitational affect that the earth has on the masses within its orbital path.

2. According to another transmission the noble Prophet mentions a scientific miracle that would be discovered long after his time. In those days, people believed that the sun and all star constellations revolved around the earth. Whereas, on the first occasion when the Prophet was asked, he replied, "The earth stands on a fish." Three months after when he was asked again, he replied, "It stands on

an ox". He was actually referring to the constellations of Pisces and Taurus.

With this scientific explanation that would be recognized in the future, he was indicating to the fact that it is not the sun that revolves around the earth but it is the earth that orbits the sun. Unfortunately, over the years the interpretations have become somewhat distorted with the influence of superstition.

---

**It is said that the Qur'an is a miracle of the Prophet. What is the mystery of the miraculous literature of the Qur'an that has been preserved for centuries?**

Miracles prove God's support for the Messengers He sent. In addition, miracles displayed by Prophets are indications of scientific and technological developments that would occur in the future. For example, Moses struck a rock with his staff, and water began to flow out of the rock; hence, this indicates the discovery of modern artesian wells. Solomon's flying throne indicates to building of modern aircrafts. Also, the way he had transported the throne of the queen of Sheba from Yemen to Damascus suggests that transportation of matter would be achieved some day. Prophet Jacob's detection of the scent of Joseph all the way from the region of Canaan when Joseph was in Egypt is a sign of a technology that would transmit scent and aroma over thousands of kilometers.

Towards the end of time, human beings will exert all of their efforts in the areas of science and technology and will obtain their power from them. The miraculous literature and eloquence of the Holy Qur'an suggests that literature and knowledge will be the most powerful tools of the future. Moreover, human beings will use the power of eloquence, literature, and expressionism to get their theories and ideologies accepted by the wider community. They will use it as a weapon to break down all arguments put forward against them.

⚬❧⚬

**Are emotions such as conscience and the sense of right and wrong developed in societies?**

Let us first take a good look at the animal kingdom. For example, there is no such a thing as a cat society. However, when nature calls, a cat does its business and then vigorously attempts to cover its droppings with earth. In which society or culture does the cat learn this? How does it make the distinction between filth and sanitation?

a. Another example is when a cat snatches a fish from the bowl. Then, the owner hits the animal on the head. The cat bows its head down and stares at the ground clearly displaying its guilt. We even have a saying for children who act this way when they misbehave, "he is like a pussy cat now." Cats often play with children's toys. When a cat breaks the toy, it quickly runs for cover. The animal knows that it has done something wrong. There is no medium in the cat kingdom for the development of such emotions.

b. Pigeons are renowned for their sense of justice and loyalty towards their mates.

c. It is common knowledge that horses remain loyal to their masters until they die.

d. If a male camel realizes that someone is watching them during mating, it moves away from its partner and in some cases chases the observer off.

An interesting event took place at the circus of Cairo in Egypt. A lion tamer named Muhammad al-Huluw sustained a fatal injury when one of his lions was jumping over his head during a show. The circus staff explains the aftermath of the unfortunate incident: "The lion abstained from eating and incarcerated itself to its cage. No matter what we did, we could not get him to eat. Finally, we decided to place him in a zoo where he could mate. However, there he attacked the female lion. The animal continued to fast while he kept on inflicting wounds on his own paw. Eventually, he starved himself to death." Where did this wild animal learn such an emotional behavior? Is there a rule in the wild which states that if you kill a human being, you must commit suicide?

Indeed, conscience is a divine light. Events that occur in social life enable this light to become more transparent and polish the carnal soul.

**What is the wisdom behind encircling the Ka'ba during Hajj and why is the *tawaf* performed seven times?**

Small bodies always orbit the larger ones. This is a general law of nature. From an electron to planets, stars, and galaxies, all matter is in motion around a larger mass. Without doubt, everything in the universe revolves around the greatest truth. The Ka'ba was the first place of worship built by Abraham. Since Abraham, it has been considered to be a sign from God or the house of God.

In respect to the significance of the number seven, what is the mystery behind the seven notes in music? It is the same case with the spectrum, there are seven colors. The electrons travel around the nuclei of the atom in seven different orbits. Let us not forget that there are seven days in a week. Humanity did not come together to decide this.

At the conclusion of each prayer, we recite Subhanallah, Alhamdulillah, and Allahu Akbar thirty-three times. Reciting certain words for a certain number of times is like mysterious keys to divine blessings.

---

**Since days and nights can last for six months in regions such as the North Pole, how are we supposed to perform our daily prayers there?**

Daily prayers should be arranged to match the prayer times of the closest region that has a normal cycle of twenty-four hours. We have to remember at such locations one also has to re-organize his/her eating, sleeping, and working times.

Is there a religious literature that supports the claim of
breaking the 24 hours into scheduled days in order to
perform prayers in regions that days and nights last for
six months?

Islam leaves no issue to dispute. Accordingly, the evidence
is in Sahih Bukhari and the Musnad of Ahmad ibn Han-
bal. The noble messenger of God discusses an issue about
time with his companions in one Hadith:

The noble Prophet said, "Dajjal will emerge when people turn away from religion." In another narration he said,
"Dajjal will emerge from the east and travel the earth in
forty days. Some of his days are like a year compared to
yours. Some are like a month, some are like a week and
some are the same as your days." The companions asked,
"Will a day's prayer be enough for the day that lasts a
year?" The noble Prophet replied, "No...you will have to
calculate and reorganize your prayers" (This means that
one would have to divide the days into twenty-four hours
and perform the prayers accordingly).

According to this Hadith, people who travel to these
regions should use the prayer calendar of the nearest
region and divide the days into twenty-four hours.
Indeed, in such regions we do not neglect our eating,
working, sleeping, and bathing habits, so we should not
neglect our worship such as the daily prayers and the
obligatory fast.

Since the astonishing creation and the awesome occurrences that take place in the universe are not a result of necessity, then what is the divine purpose behind them?

First point: When a person performs a natural or a social duty in the most enthusiastic manner, those observing him will naturally assume that the individual is performing these duties for a significant objective, a beneficial reason, or a profitable purpose. These objectives could be considered the main purpose.

Second point: There must be some form of enticement such as love, passion, or pleasure which encourages the individual to perform that duty. These purposes may be described as reasons for inducement or temptations. For example, the enticement that comes from appetite encourages us to eat. However, the real purpose of eating is to nourish the body and to survive.

Therefore, the amazing and awesome occurrences that take place in the universe happen for infinite divine reasons that emerge from two groups of Divine Names.

The first reason: The Asma al-Husna (Beautiful names of God) have many different unimaginable manifestations. This is one of the reasons there are so many different species. These beautiful names need continuous manifestation. What this means is that the manifestations of the beautiful names of God would wish to renew and refresh the pages and the letters of this great book of the universe. It is imperative that these names are manifested with new semantic meanings on letters of creation and presented initially before God, and then before the angels, the Jinn, and human beings so that they could be read and scrutinized.

THE SECOND REASON AND DIVINE WISDOM: The activities and duties performed by all creation come from an appetite or an incentive. Moreover, there is pleasure concealed within every duty; perhaps every duty is a pleasure in itself. Accordingly, there is an eternally sanctified love and infinitely sacred compassion suitable to the reality of a self-existent God, who does not need anything, whose being is unique, and who is omnipotent. In all living beings, there is a sacred desire that originates from this sacred love and compassion. Hence, this sacred desire generates a sacred joy of unimaginable proportions. In turn, this sacred joy provides an infinitely sanctified pleasure. Finally, there is immeasurable holy pleasure and pride that belongs to the All-Compassionate and the All-Merciful, and it originates from the manifestation of infinite compassion, display of power amongst the creation, the transformation of potential power to action, and from the development and materialization of perfection. Hence, this in itself needs limitless action.

Let us think about a generous, munificent, and compassionate person who prepares a wonderful feast for the poor, needy, and the starving on board a travelling ship that belongs to him. He is watching them from above. You would realize the amount of satisfaction and joy this generous individual will receive from observing the contentment, pleasure, and expressions of gratitude displayed on the faces of these needy people.

Now compare the joy of this human being who is not even the true owner of the ship or the feast to the magnificent inimitable feast prepared on this planet that resembles a ship travelling through space inhabited by human beings, jinn, and animals whose needs and desires are infinite. Not only are they invited to the feast that resembles a small breakfast but they are also invited to an eternal paradise where countless tables of various feasts and banquets prepared in a most perfect way await them. The holy meaning of the love that originates from the All-Compassionate and the All-Merciful, who answers the endless needs and desires of His servants, should be compared and contemplated according to these merciful results.

This means the thousands of beautiful divine names necessitate the creation of this universe and the magnificent art and purposeful acts that exist in it. All masterpieces created by God are scrutinized by human beings and the jinn as if they were all a magnificent book. Also, the Almighty himself observes and monitors His own glorious art. Unlike the limited contemplation of human beings and spiritual beings, He observes His creation in incredible detail. Our understanding of the purpose in the constant change and renewal we observe in God's astonishing art originates from extraordinary desire, love, will, and zeal. These descriptions may be regarded as deficiencies in human terms. Therefore, it would be incorrect to use them in reference to the Almighty because these limited molds cannot describe His infinite attributes. We would need to add terms such as, "The self-existence, Omnipotent, a Supreme Being who is beyond contemplation and who needs nothing" to our definitions.